The Seven Steps to Lasting Wealth and Emotional Security

Richard Trillion Mantey

Dedication

To those who were told they'd never make it.

To the dreamers who work in silence, the givers who pour into others without ever feeling full themselves, and the warriors who smile through invisible battles.

To my incredible parents—thank you for teaching me the value of hard work, resilience, and love.

This book is for everyone who's ever felt behind, broken, or afraid to start over.

May these words remind you: your wealth, your healing, and your breakthrough are already within you.

Keep going. You're closer than you t

Acknowledgments

Writing this book has been a journey of reflection, growth, and gratitude. I want to thank every person who helped make it possible.

To my parents—your unwavering belief in me, even when I doubted myself, has been my greatest source of strength. Your sacrifices, love, and wisdom shaped the foundation on which this book stands.

To my editor, whose sharp eye and deeper understanding helped refine each chapter—thank you for elevating this message while honoring its heart.

To my mentors, coaches, and teachers—thank you for pouring your knowledge into me. Each lesson became a step on the path I now share with others.

To my friends and readers—your encouragement and feedback have fueled my purpose. You reminded me why this message matters.

And finally, to the person holding this book: thank you for trusting me with your time and attention. I wrote this for you. May it guide you toward a life of lasting wealth and unshakable peace.

About the Author

Richard Trillion is a globally respected voice in personal finance, emotional intelligence, and success psychology. With a mission to help everyday people build unshakable wealth and inner peace, Richard draws from over a decade of experience in coaching, business strategy, and mindset transformation. His journey—from overcoming personal setbacks to achieving financial independence—has inspired thousands to take control of their lives.

Through speaking engagements, online courses, and bestselling books, Richard empowers readers with simple yet powerful strategies to unlock financial freedom while mastering their emotional world. His work blends practical money wisdom with deep inner healing—because true wealth, he believes, begins within.

When he's not writing or teaching, Richard enjoys traveling, meditating, and mentoring future leaders. The Seven Steps to Lasting Wealth and Emotional Security is his most transformative work yet—offering a step-by-step path to the financial abundance and emotional calm we all deserve.

Preface

Wealth and emotional security. Two of the most sought-after goals in life—yet so often misunderstood, and even more often, pursued separately.

Many chase financial success only to feel empty when they get there. Others focus on emotional well-being but silently struggle with financial instability. But what if the key to true fulfillment is not in choosing one over the other—but in mastering both?

The Seven Steps to Lasting Wealth and Emotional Security was born from that very question.

Over the years, I've met people from all walks of life—entrepreneurs, professionals, parents, students—who shared a common desire: to feel secure in their finances and grounded in their emotions. This book is a guide for them—and for you.

Inside, you'll discover a step-by-step framework that bridges the inner and outer worlds of success. From building smart financial habits to rewiring your mindset for abundance, each chapter is designed to bring clarity, confidence, and peace—not just in your bank account, but in your everyday life.

This isn't just another money book. It's a journey into how financial freedom and emotional well-being go hand in hand—and how, together, they create a foundation for a life of purpose, joy, and true security.

If you're ready to stop living paycheck to paycheck—mentally, emotionally, or financially—and start building real, lasting wealth from the inside out, then turn the page.

Your new story begins now.

Contents

Chapter 1: Understanding Wealth and Emotional Security

The Connection Between Wealth and Well-Being

Wealth and well-being are often seen as intertwined concepts, yet many overlook the profound impact that financial stability can have on emotional health. Consider the story of Maria, a single mother who worked multiple jobs just to make ends meet. Her struggle left her feeling exhausted and anxious, but once she began to implement smart financial decisions, her life transformed. With each small step toward financial peace, she found herself not only managing her finances better but also experiencing a deeper sense of well-being and security.

Research supports the idea that financial stability contributes significantly to emotional health. Studies reveal that individuals with a solid financial foundation tend to report higher levels of happiness and lower stress. This connection between wealth and well-being isn't just anecdotal; it's backed by science. Neuroscientists have found that the brain releases feel-good chemicals when we experience financial security, creating a positive feedback loop that enhances our overall emotional state.

To cultivate this connection between wealth and well-being, we can take deliberate steps. Start by assessing your financial situation and identifying areas for improvement. Set specific, achievable financial goals that align with your values and aspirations. As you make progress, celebrate those victories, no matter how small they may seem. This practice not only boosts your financial literacy but also enhances your emotional resilience, reinforcing the link between your financial decisions and your overall happiness.

Another powerful way to enhance well-being through wealth is by giving back. Philanthropy has been shown to elevate emotional health, as helping others creates a sense of purpose and fulfillment. For instance, John, a successful entrepreneur, found that after he started donating a portion of his income to local charities, his sense of happiness skyrocketed. The act of giving not only improved his community but also enriched his own life, illustrating the multifaceted nature of wealth and well-being.

Ultimately, the connection between wealth and well-being is a journey, not a destination. It requires ongoing reflection and commitment to making wise financial decisions. By recognizing the importance of this relationship and taking actionable steps, you can pave the way to not only financial peace but also a profound sense of emotional security. Embrace this journey, and you'll find that lasting wealth and genuine well-being go hand in hand, creating a fulfilling life that resonates beyond mere numbers.

Defining Lasting Wealth

Defining lasting wealth goes beyond mere financial accumulation; it encompasses the richness of life experiences, emotional fulfillment, and the freedom to pursue one's passions. Consider the story of Maria, a single mother who, after years of struggling, defined her wealth not just by her paycheck but by the time she could spend with her children. By prioritizing her family's happiness over material possessions, Maria discovered that true wealth includes the joy of shared moments and meaningful connections.

Science reinforces this idea, suggesting that emotional well-being is closely linked to our financial decisions. Research shows that individuals who focus on experiences rather than things report higher satisfaction levels in their lives. This reflects the shift towards valuing relationships and personal growth over the relentless pursuit of financial gain. By making conscious wealth decisions, we can cultivate a life that feels abundant in both material and emotional aspects.

The journey to lasting wealth involves three critical decisions: prioritizing experiences, fostering relationships, and practicing gratitude. Each step is essential in reshaping how we view wealth. When we choose to invest in experiences, like traveling or taking a class, we enrich our lives in ways that money alone cannot provide. These experiences create memories that last much longer than any possession, solidifying our understanding of what it means to be truly wealthy.

Building relationships also plays a vital role in defining wealth. Strong connections with family, friends, and community offer support and fulfillment that wealth cannot buy. Engaging in meaningful interactions not only enhances emotional security but also provides a robust support system during challenging times. The wealth of our relationships often determines our resilience and happiness, making it a pivotal factor in our overall sense of prosperity.

Finally, cultivating gratitude is a powerful practice in achieving lasting wealth. By recognizing and appreciating what we have, we shift our focus from what we lack to the abundance present in our lives. This mindset not only enhances our emotional well-being but also influences our financial choices positively. When we approach wealth with gratitude, we invite more opportunities for growth and joy, ultimately leading to a more fulfilling life that embodies the essence of lasting wealth.

The Role of Emotional Security in Financial Health

Emotional security plays a pivotal role in our financial health, often serving as the foundation upon which we build our monetary decisions. When individuals feel secure emotionally, they tend to approach financial matters with clarity and confidence. For instance, consider a story of a young woman named Sarah who, after overcoming her anxiety related to money, was able to create a budget and save for her first home. By addressing her emotional hurdles, she transformed her financial landscape, showcasing the profound impact that emotional well-being can have on financial decisions.

Research indicates that emotional security can significantly influence our spending habits and investment choices. Studies show that individuals with high emotional resilience are more likely to engage in long-term financial planning, as they are less swayed by impulsive decisions driven by fear or insecurity. This was true for John, a father of two, who learned to manage his stress through mindfulness techniques. As a result, he made informed investment choices that ensured his family's financial future, demonstrating the correlation between emotional well-being and financial stability.

The steps toward achieving both emotional security and financial health are interconnected. First, it's crucial to develop self-awareness regarding one's financial triggers. Keeping a journal can help track emotions tied to spending or saving. For example, Maria, a small business owner, began journaling and discovered that her urge to splurge came during stressful weeks. By addressing the source of her stress through healthier outlets, she reduced her impulsive spending, thus reinforcing her financial security.

Additionally, building a support system can foster emotional security, which in turn enhances financial health. Engaging with a community or seeking mentorship can provide encouragement and accountability. A poignant example lies with a group of friends who formed a financial accountability circle. They shared their struggles and successes, ultimately creating a safe space where they could openly discuss their financial goals without judgment. This collective emotional support not only improved their financial literacy but also deepened their friendships.

Ultimately, cultivating emotional security is not just about feeling good; it's about empowering ourselves to make informed financial decisions that lead to lasting wealth. By integrating emotional health practices into our financial planning, we can create a more stable and prosperous future. The stories of individuals like Sarah, John, and Maria serve as reminders that the journey towards financial peace is often as much about emotional resilience as it is about numbers.

Chapter 2: The Mindset of Abundance

Shifting from Scarcity to Abundance

The transition from a mindset of scarcity to one of abundance is a powerful journey that can change not only our financial circumstances but also our emotional well-being. Many people grow up with the belief that there is never enough—enough money, enough love, or enough opportunities. This belief can lead to anxiety and a constant feeling of lack. However, by shifting our perspective to see the abundance that already exists in our lives, we can unlock a world of possibilities and create lasting wealth.

Consider the story of Sarah, a single mother who struggled to make ends meet. For years, she believed that her financial struggles defined her worth. One day, while volunteering at a local shelter, she realized that her time and compassion were valuable commodities. This experience opened her eyes to the abundance of love and support in her community. By embracing this mindset, Sarah not only improved her financial situation but also found a deeper sense of purpose and fulfillment.

Science backs the notion that our mindset can significantly impact our financial outcomes. Research in psychology shows that those who adopt an abundance mindset are more likely to take calculated risks, invest in themselves, and seek out new opportunities. This is because they believe in the possibility of growth and success rather than being held back by fear and limitation. By understanding this science, we can consciously choose to foster an abundance mentality in our lives.

To facilitate this shift, it's essential to take actionable steps. Start by practicing gratitude daily. Acknowledging the things you have, no matter how small, can help rewire your brain to focus on abundance rather than lack. Additionally, surround yourself with people who embody an abundance mindset. Their energy and outlook can inspire and motivate you to see the possibilities that lie ahead.

Ultimately, shifting from scarcity to abundance is not just about money; it's about creating a rich, fulfilling life. By recognizing the wealth of resources, opportunities, and love around us, we can cultivate emotional security and financial peace. Embracing this mindset allows us to navigate life's challenges with resilience and optimism, paving the way for a brighter, more prosperous future.

Overcoming Limiting Beliefs about Money

Many of us carry limiting beliefs about money that stem from our upbringing, culture, and past experiences. For instance, a common belief is that money is inherently evil or that rich people are greedy. This mindset can prevent us from seeing money as a tool for freedom and security. By acknowledging these beliefs, we can begin the process of rewriting our money story and opening ourselves to new possibilities.

Consider the story of Sarah, who grew up in a household where money was always a source of stress. She believed that making more money meant sacrificing her values and relationships. When she finally recognized this limiting belief, she sought guidance from a financial coach. Together, they reframed her perception of money, helping her see it as a means to support her loved ones and contribute to her community.

Science shows that our beliefs significantly influence our behaviors and decisions. A study published in the Journal of Personality and Social Psychology found that individuals who view money positively tend to make better financial decisions. By changing our mindset about money, we not only improve our financial literacy but also enhance our emotional well-being. The key is to challenge negative beliefs and replace them with empowering thoughts.

To overcome limiting beliefs about money, start by identifying and writing down your beliefs. Reflect on where these beliefs originated and how they have impacted your financial decisions. Next, practice affirmations that promote a healthy relationship with money, such as "Money is a tool that I can use to create the life I desire." Surround yourself with positive influences, such as books, podcasts, and mentors who share a mindset of abundance.

Lastly, take actionable steps to demonstrate your new beliefs. This could involve setting financial goals, creating a budget, or investing in your education. As you take these steps, notice how your feelings about money shift.

Remember, overcoming limiting beliefs about money is a journey, but with persistence and the right mindset, you can unlock financial peace and emotional security.

Cultivating a Growth-Oriented Perspective

Cultivating a growth-oriented perspective is essential for achieving lasting wealth and emotional security. This mindset encourages individuals to view challenges as opportunities rather than obstacles. For example, consider the story of a young entrepreneur who faced repeated failures in launching his startup. Instead of giving up, he analyzed each setback, learned from his mistakes, and ultimately found success, illustrating how resilience can lead to financial peace.

Research supports the idea that a growth mindset can significantly impact one's financial decisions. Studies have shown that individuals who embrace challenges and seek feedback tend to make better financial choices. They are more likely to invest in their education and seek out new opportunities, rather than sticking to the familiar, which can often lead to stagnation. This scientific backing emphasizes the importance of shifting our focus from a fixed to a growth mindset.

To cultivate this perspective, it is crucial to adopt specific strategies. First, set clear, achievable goals that stretch your capabilities. For instance, if you aim to save a certain amount of money, break that goal into smaller, manageable steps. Celebrate each small victory to keep your motivation high.

Additionally, surround yourself with positive influences—people who encourage growth and challenge you to think differently about your financial decisions.

Another effective step is to embrace lifelong learning. Financial literacy is not a one-time lesson but an ongoing journey. Attend workshops, read books, and engage in discussions about personal finance. This knowledge equips you to make informed decisions and adapt to changing circumstances. A commitment to learning fosters resilience and helps you stay ahead in the ever-evolving financial landscape.

Finally, practice self-compassion during setbacks. Recognize that everyone encounters difficulties on their path to wealth and emotional security. Instead of dwelling on failures, treat them as invaluable lessons. By maintaining a growth-oriented perspective, you will build the emotional resilience necessary for long-term financial success, ultimately leading to peace and security in your life.

Chapter 3: The Importance of Financial Literacy

Basic Financial Concepts Everyone Should Know

Understanding basic financial concepts is crucial for anyone seeking to achieve lasting wealth and emotional security. One of the first concepts to grasp is the difference between assets and liabilities. An asset is something that puts money in your pocket, like investments or rental properties, while a liability takes money out, such as loans or credit card debt. For example, consider Jane, who invested in stocks that appreciated over time. Meanwhile, her friend Mark took on debt to purchase a new car, which soon lost value. By focusing on acquiring assets, Jane has built a solid financial foundation, demonstrating the importance of this concept.

Another fundamental idea is the power of compound interest. This principle allows your money to grow exponentially over time, as interest earns interest. Take the story of Tom, who started investing just $50 a month in his early twenties. By the time he reached retirement, his small contributions had grown into a substantial nest egg, thanks to the magic of compounding. Understanding this concept can motivate individuals to start saving early, even if the amounts seem small at first, reinforcing the idea that every little bit counts.

Budgeting is also a critical skill that everyone should master. Creating a budget helps you track your income and expenses, allowing for better financial decision-making.

Sarah, for instance, found herself overwhelmed with bills until she decided to create a monthly budget. By categorizing her spending and setting limits, she not only reduced her expenses but also discovered money to allocate towards her savings. This story illustrates how budgeting can empower individuals to take control of their financial lives and work towards their goals.

It's essential to recognize the importance of an emergency fund as part of financial planning. Life is unpredictable, and having savings set aside for unexpected expenses can prevent financial stress. When Michael's car broke down unexpectedly, he was able to cover the repair costs without resorting to credit cards, thanks to his emergency fund. This experience highlights how having a financial safety net can provide peace of mind and emotional security in times of uncertainty.

Finally, understanding the concept of financial literacy is vital for making informed decisions. It encompasses knowledge about budgeting, saving, investing, and understanding credit. When Lisa took the initiative to educate herself about personal finance, she transformed her financial situation. She learned how to negotiate her salary and invest wisely, ultimately leading her to financial independence. Lisa's journey emphasizes the power of knowledge and the importance of continuous learning in achieving lasting wealth and emotional security.

Understanding Investments and Returns

Investments are not just a means to grow wealth; they are a pathway to financial peace and emotional security. Picture a single mother, Sarah, who saved diligently over the years. She invested in a diverse portfolio, including stocks and bonds, and watched her small savings blossom over time. Sarah's story demonstrates that investments, when approached with knowledge and care, can turn dreams into reality, providing a safety net for herself and her children.

Understanding returns on investments is crucial for anyone looking to build lasting wealth. Returns represent the profit made from investments, and they come in various forms—interest, dividends, or capital gains. For instance, a young entrepreneur, Alex, invested in a tech startup. After several years, his patience paid off as the company's value soared, resulting in significant returns. Alex's experience underscores the importance of not only making investments but also understanding their potential returns to make informed decisions.

The science of investing is grounded in principles that can be learned and applied by anyone. Behavioral finance shows how emotions influence investment choices, often leading to poor decision-making. By understanding these psychological factors, individuals can develop strategies to combat emotional biases. Consider the story of Maria, who, after facing losses during a market downturn, educated herself on market cycles and re-entered with confidence. Her journey illustrates that knowledge can empower investors to remain resilient and make choices based on logic rather than fear.

To embark on a successful investment journey, one must take actionable steps. First, set clear financial goals to guide your investment choices. Next, educate yourself about different asset classes and their risks. Lastly, diversify your investments to mitigate potential losses. Take the example of John, who began with a simple savings account but, through diligent research and planning, built a robust investment portfolio. His systematic approach highlights that lasting wealth is not a matter of luck but a result of informed decisions and consistent effort.

In conclusion, understanding investments and returns is vital for achieving financial peace and emotional security. By learning from real-life stories and applying scientific principles, anyone can navigate the complex world of investing. Remember, every successful investor started as a novice. With the right education and mindset, you too can unlock the doors to lasting wealth and emotional well-being, just like Sarah, Alex, Maria, and John did on their journeys.

Navigating Debt and Credit

Navigating debt and credit can often feel like traversing a labyrinth, especially when emotions run high and financial decisions weigh heavily on our minds. Many people find themselves in situations where credit cards and loans seem to spiral out of control, leading to stress and anxiety. Take the story of Maria, a single mother who fell into debt after unexpected medical expenses. Her journey through financial turmoil taught her invaluable lessons about managing credit, which can resonate with many in similar situations.

Understanding the science behind debt is crucial. Research shows that emotional responses to financial stress can cloud judgment, leading to poor decision-making. For instance, when faced with mounting bills, individuals often resort to quick fixes like payday loans, which can lead to even deeper financial holes. It's essential to recognize these patterns and approach financial decisions with a clear mind. Maria learned to pause and assess her options, which marked the turning point in her journey toward financial stability.

The first step in navigating debt is to create a comprehensive budget that outlines income and expenses. This step provides clarity and helps prioritize debt repayment. Maria used a simple spreadsheet to track her spending, which revealed where she could cut back. By reallocating funds, she was able to put more money toward her debts. This practical approach is a strategy supported by financial experts who emphasize the importance of budgeting as a foundational tool for managing debt effectively.

Next, understanding the nuances of credit scores is vital. A good credit score can open doors to better loan terms and lower interest rates, while a poor score can trap individuals in a cycle of high-interest debt. Maria took the initiative to educate herself about credit scores, learning how her actions, like timely payments and maintaining low credit utilization, could positively impact her financial health. This knowledge empowered her to make informed decisions that would benefit her long-term stability.

Finally, seek support from financial advisors or peer groups. Sharing experiences and strategies can provide much-needed encouragement and insight. Maria found solace in a community group where members shared their stories and solutions. This network helped her stay motivated and accountable on her journey. As you navigate your own debt and credit landscape, remember that seeking help is a sign of strength, and it can lead to lasting financial peace.

Chapter 4: Creating a Sustainable Budget

The Essentials of Budgeting

Budgeting is the cornerstone of financial health and emotional security. It starts with understanding where your money comes from and where it goes. Many people find themselves overwhelmed by expenses that seem to multiply, yet they often overlook the power of a well-structured budget. By tracking income and expenditures, individuals can take control of their finances, making conscious choices that align with their values and goals. The journey of budgeting is not just about numbers; it's about creating a life you love without financial stress.

Consider the story of Sarah, a single mother who struggled to make ends meet. By implementing a simple budgeting method, she began to categorize her expenses into needs and wants. This approach not only helped her prioritize essential spending but also revealed areas where she could save. Over time, Sarah built an emergency fund and even started to save for her children's education. Her transformation from anxiety to confidence illustrates how effective budgeting can change lives.

Science supports the notion that budgeting can lead to better financial decisions and less stress. Studies show that individuals who actively manage their finances report higher levels of satisfaction and lower levels of anxiety. This psychological benefit arises from the sense of control and clarity that a budget provides. When people know their financial situation, they can make informed choices, whether it's saving for a vacation or investing in their future.

To create an effective budget, start by listing all sources of income and monthly expenses. Next, categorize your expenses to identify where adjustments can be made. Allocate funds to savings, debt repayment, and discretionary spending, ensuring your priorities reflect your values. Review your budget regularly to adapt to changes in income or expenses, and remember that budgeting is a dynamic process that evolves with your financial journey.

In conclusion, mastering the essentials of budgeting is crucial for achieving lasting wealth and emotional security. It empowers individuals to make informed financial decisions, reduce stress, and ultimately create a life aligned with their dreams. By embracing budgeting, you are not just managing your money; you are taking a significant step towards financial peace and a fulfilling life.

Identifying Needs vs. Wants

In the journey towards financial peace and emotional security, understanding the difference between needs and wants is crucial. Needs are essentials for survival—food, shelter, clothing—while wants are the luxuries that enhance our lives but are not necessary for our existence. A story that illustrates this distinction is that of Sarah, a single mother who, after losing her job, had to prioritize her limited resources. She learned to focus on what was essential for her and her children, which helped her regain control over her finances and ultimately led her to a more stable situation.

Scientific research supports the idea that distinguishing between needs and wants can lead to better financial decisions. Behavioral economists have found that people often fall into the trap of conflating their wants with their needs, leading to overspending and financial stress. By clearly categorizing expenses, individuals can allocate their budgets wisely. For instance, when John decided to track his spending, he realized that many of his daily coffee runs were wants that he could easily cut back on, freeing up funds for more pressing needs like savings and debt repayment.

The first step in identifying needs versus wants is to create a comprehensive list of your expenses. Once you have this list, categorize each item into needs and wants. This exercise can be eye-opening, as many people discover that they spend a significant amount of money on things they want rather than what they truly need. Reflecting on this list can motivate individuals to make more informed choices about their spending habits, ultimately contributing to their financial well-being.

Another effective strategy is to implement the "30-day rule" for wants. If you see something you want, wait 30 days before purchasing it. This pause allows you to evaluate whether the item is genuinely necessary or just a fleeting desire. Many people find that after a month, they no longer feel the urge to buy the item, which saves them money and reinforces the habit of prioritizing needs over wants.

Ultimately, the distinction between needs and wants is not just about financial management; it's about fostering a mindset of gratitude and contentment. When you focus on fulfilling your needs first, you create a solid foundation for financial peace. This shift in perspective can transform your relationship with money, helping you to cultivate emotional security. As Sarah, John, and many others have discovered, identifying needs versus wants is a powerful step towards lasting wealth and a more fulfilled life.

Tools and Techniques for Effective Budgeting

Effective budgeting is not just about tracking expenses; it's a mindset that empowers individuals to take control of their financial futures. The journey begins with understanding your financial landscape—knowing how much you earn, where your money goes, and what your financial goals are. A compelling story is that of Sarah, a single mother who, after facing overwhelming debt, decided to embrace budgeting as a tool for change. By analyzing her income and expenses, she realized that small adjustments could lead to significant savings, ultimately allowing her to build a safety net for her children.

One essential technique for effective budgeting is the envelope system, which uses physical envelopes for different spending categories. This method not only limits overspending but also provides a tangible way to visualize your financial boundaries. For example, John, an avid diner, allocated a specific amount to his dining envelope. By being mindful of his spending, he learned to appreciate meals at home while still enjoying the occasional restaurant visit. Such strategies foster discipline and awareness, making budgeting a rewarding experience rather than a chore.

Incorporating technology into budgeting can enhance clarity and efficiency. Numerous apps and tools allow users to track their expenses in real-time, categorize spending, and set financial goals. For instance, Lisa, a recent college graduate, discovered a budgeting app that helped her stay on top of her student loans and living expenses. With notifications and visual progress reports, she could celebrate her milestones, reinforcing positive financial habits. This blend of technology and personal finance not only simplifies budgeting but also makes it engaging and interactive.

Another crucial component of effective budgeting is regular review and adjustment. Life circumstances change, and so do financial priorities. Mark, a small business owner, found that reviewing his budget monthly helped him adapt to fluctuating income and unexpected expenses. By analyzing his budget regularly, he identified areas for improvement and took proactive steps to align his spending with his evolving goals. This ongoing process cultivates resilience and adaptability, essential traits for anyone on the path to financial peace.

Lastly, emotional factors play a significant role in budgeting. Understanding the psychological barriers to saving and spending can provide insights into one's financial behaviors. Maria, who struggled with impulse purchases, sought the help of a financial coach. Through guided reflection, she learned to connect her spending habits with her emotions, ultimately leading to healthier financial choices. Recognizing the emotional aspects of budgeting transforms it into an empowering journey toward lasting wealth and emotional security.

Chapter 5: Building Multiple Income Streams

The Benefits of Diversification

Diversification is a fundamental principle that can lead to financial stability and peace of mind. Imagine a farmer who grows only one type of crop; if a disease strikes that crop, the farmer faces ruin. However, if that same farmer diversifies their crops—growing vegetables, fruits, and grains—they can weather the storms of nature and market fluctuations. This story illustrates how spreading risk across different investments can protect and enhance your financial future.

Science backs the power of diversification. Numerous studies show that a diversified portfolio reduces volatility and increases the chances of better returns over time. For instance, research from financial experts reveals that investors who diversify their assets across stocks, bonds, and real estate tend to outperform those who put all their money into a single investment. This is because, while one asset class may underperform, others may thrive, balancing out potential losses.

To implement diversification effectively, start by assessing your current financial situation. Take stock of your investments and consider how they are allocated. Are you heavily weighted in one area? If so, it might be time to explore opportunities in other sectors or asset classes. Simple steps, like investing in index funds or mutual funds, can provide instant diversification without the need for extensive research.

Emotional security plays a crucial role in financial decision-making. When investors know their money is spread across various assets, they feel more secure and less likely to panic during market downturns. This sense of stability allows for better decision-making and reduces the emotional toll that financial uncertainty can have on individuals. The story of a retiree who diversified their investments illustrates this point; they enjoyed their retirement years without the anxiety of market fluctuations affecting their lifestyle.

In conclusion, diversification is not just a strategy; it's a mindset that can lead to lasting wealth and emotional security. By understanding its importance, applying the principles of diversification to your investments, and embracing the peace of mind it brings, you can unlock financial freedom. Remember, just as a diverse garden flourishes, so too will your financial life when you cultivate a variety of investments.

Exploring Passive Income Opportunities

In today's fast-paced world, the quest for financial stability often leads individuals to explore passive income opportunities. Imagine a woman named Sarah, who, after years of working tirelessly, discovered the power of earning money while she slept. She invested in rental properties, allowing her to generate income without actively working every hour of the day. This kind of financial freedom is attainable for anyone willing to research and take actionable steps towards creating multiple streams of income.

The science behind passive income is rooted in the idea of leveraging your resources—whether they be time, money, or skills—to create wealth. Studies show that individuals who diversify their income sources are less stressed about financial uncertainties. This is evident in the story of Mark, who turned his passion for photography into a thriving online course. By teaching others what he loved, he not only generated income but also built a community around his passion, proving that passive income can align with personal interests.

To embark on your journey toward passive income, start by assessing your skills and resources. What do you enjoy doing? What knowledge do you possess that others may find valuable? Once you identify these areas, the next step is to research potential opportunities. For instance, online platforms allow you to create and sell digital products, from eBooks to courses, making it easier than ever to reach a global audience. Taking small, deliberate steps can lead to significant financial gains over time.

It's also essential to understand the importance of patience and persistence in building a passive income stream. Consider the story of Lisa, who started a blog as a side project. Initially, her income was modest, but she continued refining her content and engaging with her audience. Over time, her blog became a source of significant revenue through affiliate marketing and sponsorships. Lisa's experience serves as a testament to the fact that success in passive income requires dedication and a long-term perspective.

In conclusion, exploring passive income opportunities can be a transformative journey towards financial peace and emotional security. By learning from the experiences of others, leveraging your unique skills, and remaining patient, you can unlock the door to lasting wealth. The first step begins with a decision to act, paving the way for a more secure and fulfilling financial future.

Leveraging Skills and Talents for Extra Income

In today's world, leveraging your skills and talents can open doors to extra income opportunities that were previously unimaginable. Many people have turned their hobbies into profitable ventures, discovering not just financial benefits but also a renewed sense of purpose. For instance, consider the story of Sarah, who transformed her passion for baking into a thriving online business. She started by selling her homemade goods to friends and family, and before long, her delectable treats gained popularity on social media, leading to a significant side income.

Understanding your unique skills is the first step toward monetizing them. Reflect on what you enjoy doing and what you excel at. This could range from artistic skills like painting or graphic design to practical talents such as carpentry or coding. Research shows that individuals who engage in activities aligned with their passions often experience higher levels of satisfaction and fulfillment. This emotional connection can fuel your drive to succeed, making the journey toward extra income not just profitable, but also enjoyable.

Next, consider the various platforms available for showcasing your talents. Websites like Etsy or Upwork provide a marketplace for creatives and freelancers alike. By creating a profile and marketing your services or products effectively, you can tap into a global audience. Take the example of Mark, a freelance writer who started his career on a small freelance platform. With dedication and skill, he expanded his client base and now enjoys financial freedom while working from anywhere in the world.

Networking is another crucial element in leveraging your skills for income. Connecting with like-minded individuals can provide support, inspiration, and collaboration opportunities. Attend workshops, seminars, or online webinars related to your field. By building a community, you can exchange ideas, discover new opportunities, and even find potential partners for joint ventures. The story of a group of artists who formed a collective to promote their work exemplifies the power of collaboration in achieving financial goals.

Finally, remember that persistence is key. The path to leveraging your skills for extra income may have its challenges, but perseverance will pay off. Set realistic goals and track your progress. Celebrate small victories along the way, as they will motivate you to keep pushing forward. With the right mindset, dedication, and support, you can turn your skills into a reliable source of income, ultimately leading to greater financial peace and emotional security.

Chapter 6: The Power of Saving and Investing

Strategies for Smart Saving

Saving money is not just about putting aside a portion of your income; it's about adopting a mindset that prioritizes financial security. Many people are caught in the cycle of spending without thinking about the long-term consequences of their decisions. For instance, consider the story of Sarah, a young professional who constantly dined out and bought the latest gadgets. It wasn't until she faced an unexpected medical bill that she realized the importance of having savings. By changing her spending habits and focusing on saving, she turned her financial situation around, illustrating that small adjustments can lead to significant outcomes.

One effective strategy for smart saving is to automate your savings. By setting up automatic transfers from your checking account to a savings account, you can ensure that saving becomes a part of your monthly routine. Research shows that people who automate their savings are more likely to reach their financial goals than those who rely on willpower alone. Imagine waking up each month knowing that your savings have grown without you having to think about it. This simple step can relieve the stress associated with budgeting and help create a more secure financial future.

Another important strategy is to set specific, measurable savings goals. Instead of a vague intention to save more, specify how much you want to save and by when. For example, if you aim to save for a vacation, determine the total amount needed and break it down into monthly contributions. This method mirrors the scientific principle of goal-setting theory, which suggests that specific goals lead to better performance. By having a clear target, you can stay motivated and track your progress, making the journey to financial peace feel attainable.

Additionally, consider implementing the 50/30/20 rule for budgeting, where 50% of your income goes to needs, 30% to wants, and 20% to savings. This framework helps create a balanced approach to managing your finances. John, a father of two, adopted this strategy after realizing he was overspending on non-essential items. By reallocating his budget, he not only increased his savings but also reduced financial stress within his family. This practical approach can help anyone feel more in control and secure about their financial future.

Lastly, always remember the power of community and support in your saving journey. Sharing your goals with friends or joining a savings group can provide encouragement and accountability. Studies have shown that social support significantly enhances motivation and success in achieving financial goals. For example, a group of friends committed to saving for a shared goal found themselves more disciplined and inspired. Surrounding yourself with like-minded individuals can make the path to financial security less daunting and more enjoyable, fostering a sense of camaraderie in the pursuit of wealth and emotional security.

Understanding Different Investment Vehicles

In today's complex financial landscape, understanding different investment vehicles is crucial for anyone seeking lasting wealth and emotional security. Investment vehicles range from traditional options like stocks and bonds to more contemporary choices such as real estate and cryptocurrencies. Each vehicle has its own risk profile, potential returns, and unique characteristics that cater to diverse financial goals. For instance, while stocks offer the potential for high returns, they also come with significant volatility. It's essential to assess what aligns with your financial aspirations and risk tolerance.

Consider the story of Maria, a single mother who turned her modest savings into a thriving investment portfolio. Initially overwhelmed by various options, she took the time to educate herself about different investment vehicles. Through diligent research and networking with financial advisors, she discovered mutual funds, which offered her the diversification she needed without the stress of managing individual stocks. Maria's journey illustrates how knowledge and the right resources can empower anyone to navigate the investment landscape successfully.

Science backs the notion that diversifying investments can mitigate risks and enhance overall returns. Research shows that a well-balanced portfolio, which includes a mix of asset classes such as equities, fixed income, and alternative investments, can withstand market fluctuations better than one heavily weighted in a single asset. By understanding the science behind these investment vehicles, individuals can make informed decisions that align with their long-term financial strategies, ultimately leading to a more secure future.

Taking actionable steps is vital to harness the power of different investment vehicles. Start by setting clear financial goals—whether it's funding your child's education, buying a home, or preparing for retirement. Next, assess your risk tolerance and time horizon, which will guide your choice of investments. For instance, younger investors may lean towards stocks for growth, while those nearing retirement might prefer bonds for stability. Developing a strategic plan that includes regular assessments of your investments will help ensure you stay on track toward achieving your financial dreams.

Ultimately, understanding different investment vehicles is not just about numbers; it's about creating a life of financial peace and emotional security. Each decision you make today shapes your tomorrow. By learning from stories like Maria's and applying scientific principles to your investment strategy, you can cultivate a resilient portfolio that supports your aspirations. Remember, the journey to lasting wealth begins with informed choices and a commitment to continuous learning.

The Impact of Compound Interest

The concept of compound interest can be a game-changer in one's financial journey. Imagine a young individual who starts investing just $100 a month at the age of 25. By the time they reach 65, thanks to the power of compound interest, that modest investment could grow to over $1 million. This phenomenon showcases how small, consistent actions can lead to monumental outcomes over time, urging us to take our financial decisions seriously and start early.

Science backs the notion that our brains are wired to underestimate the impact of compounding. Behavioral economists have found that people often struggle to grasp exponential growth. This misunderstanding can lead to missed opportunities, as many wait too long to invest, thinking they have time on their side. By sharing stories of those who embraced the power of compounding early, we can inspire others to act sooner rather than later, highlighting that every dollar saved today can blossom into a brighter financial future.

Consider the story of Sarah, a single mother who, despite her challenges, decided to invest in her future. She set aside a small amount from her paycheck every month, which she initially thought was insignificant. However, over the years, her disciplined approach paid off, and she was able to fund her children's education without debt. Sarah's journey illustrates that compound interest is not just a financial tool; it is also a pathway to achieving dreams and securing emotional well-being.

The steps to harness the power of compound interest are straightforward. First, start by setting clear financial goals. Next, create a budget that allows for consistent contributions to savings or investment accounts. Finally, educate yourself about different investment options that can maximize returns over time. By following these steps, you can cultivate a mindset that embraces the long-term benefits of compounding, unlocking financial peace and emotional security.

In conclusion, understanding the impact of compound interest is crucial for anyone seeking financial stability. It's not merely about saving money; it's about transforming your financial landscape through informed decisions. As we share these insights, let us encourage a global audience to recognize that every small step today can lead to significant progress tomorrow, reinforcing the idea that the journey to wealth and emotional security starts with a single investment in oneself.

Chapter 7: Protecting Your Wealth

The Importance of Insurance and Risk Management

Insurance and risk management are fundamental pillars in the journey toward financial peace. Imagine a family who, after years of diligent saving, finds themselves facing an unexpected catastrophe—a house fire that destroys everything they've worked for. Without adequate insurance, this family would not only struggle to rebuild their home but also face a prolonged emotional and financial turmoil. Insurance acts as a safety net, allowing individuals and families to recover from the unforeseen circumstances that life often throws our way.

The science of risk management teaches us that risks are an inevitable part of life, whether they come in the form of health issues, natural disasters, or economic downturns. Consider the story of a small business owner who invested her life savings into her dream venture. When a sudden economic shift threatened her profits, she realized she had not protected her business with the necessary insurance. This oversight almost led to her bankruptcy. By understanding and managing risks through insurance, individuals can make informed decisions that safeguard their financial future and emotional well-being.

Steps toward effective risk management begin with assessing personal risks and understanding what insurance products are available. For instance, life insurance, health insurance, and property insurance serve different purposes, yet all contribute to a comprehensive safety strategy. By taking the time to evaluate one's situation and consulting with financial advisors, individuals can tailor their insurance plans to fit their unique needs, thus ensuring that they are prepared for whatever life may bring.

Moreover, the emotional security that comes from having a solid insurance plan cannot be overstated. Knowing that you are protected against major financial setbacks allows you to invest in your future with confidence. A couple who purchased health insurance prior to starting a family found peace of mind, knowing that their healthcare costs would not derail their dreams. This emotional stability can lead to better decision-making in other areas of life, reinforcing the idea that risk management is not just a financial tool but a pathway to a more secure and fulfilling existence.

Ultimately, the importance of insurance and risk management extends beyond personal finance; it creates a ripple effect that can strengthen communities. When families are protected, they are more likely to contribute positively to their neighborhoods, supporting local businesses and fostering connections. By prioritizing insurance and risk management, we can build a resilient society, one where individuals can thrive emotionally and financially, unlocking lasting wealth and security for generations to come.

Building an Emergency Fund

Building an emergency fund is a crucial step toward financial peace and emotional security. Imagine facing an unexpected job loss or a medical emergency without a safety net. The fear and stress that accompany such situations can be overwhelming, but having an emergency fund can provide a buffer against life's uncertainties. It transforms the way we respond to crises, allowing us to navigate them with resilience and confidence.

Scientific studies show that individuals with emergency savings experience significantly less financial anxiety. In a survey conducted by the American Psychological Association, nearly 60% of respondents cited financial stress as their primary source of worry. By establishing an emergency fund, you not only protect yourself from immediate financial distress but also improve your overall mental well-being. It's a simple step that has profound effects on your emotional health.

So how do you build this essential fund? Start by setting a clear goal. Aim to save three to six months' worth of living expenses. Break this goal down into manageable steps. For instance, if your monthly expenses are $2,000, your target should be between $6,000 and $12,000. Now, consider ways to cut back on discretionary spending. Small sacrifices, like dining out less or canceling unused subscriptions, can add up over time and help you reach your goal faster.

Next, automate your savings. Set up a separate savings account dedicated solely to your emergency fund.

Automating transfers from your checking account can make saving easier and less stressful. This way, you prioritize your future financial health without having to think about it constantly. Each month, you'll feel a sense of accomplishment as your savings grow, reinforcing the positive habit of saving.

Lastly, share your journey with friends or family. Telling others about your goal can create a support system that encourages accountability. Perhaps a friend will join you in the challenge, and together, you can celebrate your milestones. Building an emergency fund is not just about money; it's about creating a sense of security and peace in your life, allowing you to face the future with optimism and readiness.

Planning for Retirement and Future Needs

Planning for retirement is not just about accumulating wealth; it's about envisioning a future where you can live comfortably and pursue your passions. Consider the story of Maria, who dedicated her life to teaching. She spent years saving diligently, but it wasn't until she took a step back to assess her dreams that she realized she wanted to travel and volunteer in different communities. This revelation shifted her saving strategy, emphasizing the importance of aligning financial goals with personal aspirations.

Research shows that having a clear vision for retirement significantly impacts financial planning. A study by the American Psychological Association found that individuals with defined retirement goals are more likely to save effectively. This highlights that emotional security in retirement stems not only from financial stability but also from fulfilling life experiences. By creating a vision board or writing down retirement dreams, individuals can better connect with their motivations, making the saving process more meaningful.

Taking actionable steps toward your future needs is essential. Start by calculating how much you will need to live the retirement lifestyle you desire. Tools like retirement calculators can provide a solid estimate, but remember to factor in healthcare costs, potential travel, and hobbies. Additionally, consulting with a financial advisor can help tailor a plan that fits your unique circumstances, ensuring you are not just prepared financially but also emotionally for this new chapter of life.

It's important to revisit and adjust your plans regularly. Like the story of John, who had to pivot his retirement strategy when he faced unexpected health issues, flexibility is key. Life circumstances can change, and your retirement plan should be able to accommodate those changes. Keeping an open line of communication with loved ones about your plans can also create a support system that ensures you are not navigating this journey alone.

Ultimately, planning for retirement is about crafting a life that resonates with your values and dreams. By integrating financial strategies with emotional intentions, you can create a fulfilling retirement. Remember that the journey is just as important as the destination, and by taking these steps now, you are setting the foundation for a future rich in both wealth and emotional security.

Chapter 8: The Role of Relationships in Wealth Building

Communicating About Money with Partners

Communicating about money with partners is crucial for building a strong and lasting relationship. Many couples find that financial discussions can lead to tension and misunderstandings, often stemming from differing backgrounds and values regarding money. For instance, consider the story of Sarah and John, who both entered their marriage with vastly different financial experiences. Sarah grew up in a household where saving was prioritized, while John's family often indulged in spending without restraint. Their initial conversations about finances were fraught with conflict until they learned to express their values and concerns openly.

Understanding the emotional underpinnings of financial discussions can significantly improve communication. Research shows that money is often intertwined with identity and self-worth, making it a sensitive topic. When partners discuss finances, they must approach the conversation with empathy and curiosity. For example, when Sarah and John started to listen to each other's perspectives without judgment, they discovered that their differing views on money were rooted in their unique life experiences. This realization transformed their discussions from confrontational to collaborative.

Setting clear financial goals together is an essential step in fostering a healthy dialogue about money. This not only aligns partners on their financial journey but also creates a shared vision for the future. Sarah and John decided to sit down and outline their goals—saving for a home, planning vacations, and establishing an emergency fund. By articulating these shared objectives, they found common ground and a sense of partnership that had previously eluded them.

Another effective approach is to establish regular check-ins about finances. These meetings can serve as a safe space to discuss spending habits, budget adjustments, and any financial concerns. Sarah and John implemented a monthly financial date night, where they would review their budget over dinner. This ritual not only kept them accountable but also turned financial discussions into an opportunity for bonding and growth. The science behind this practice shows that couples who communicate regularly about finances tend to experience less stress and more satisfaction in their relationships.

Ultimately, the key to communicating about money with partners lies in fostering an environment of trust and openness. It's essential to remember that money discussions are not just about numbers; they are about understanding each other's values and aspirations. By approaching these conversations with vulnerability and respect, couples can navigate their financial paths together, turning potential conflicts into opportunities for connection. Sarah and John's journey illustrates that with the right tools and mindset, couples can achieve both financial peace and emotional security together.

Networking and Building Supportive Communities

In today's interconnected world, networking is not just a strategy; it is a lifeline to building supportive communities that foster both wealth and emotional security. Consider the story of Sarah, a young entrepreneur who started her business from her small apartment. By attending local meetups and engaging with other business owners, she was able to exchange ideas, gain referrals, and find mentors who guided her through the challenges of entrepreneurship. This illustrates how vital it is to create and nurture relationships that can lead to opportunities for growth and support.

Research shows that social connections can significantly impact our well-being, enhancing our emotional health and even our financial success. A study published in the American Journal of Sociology highlighted that individuals with strong social networks are more likely to achieve their goals, both personal and financial. By surrounding ourselves with supportive individuals, we create an environment that encourages risk-taking and innovation, essential components for lasting wealth.

Building a community requires intentional effort. Start by identifying the circles you wish to engage with, whether they are professional associations, local clubs, or online forums. Attend events, volunteer, or join discussions to meet like-minded individuals. As you develop these connections, share your goals and aspirations openly; vulnerability can foster deeper relationships. Remember, every connection you make is a potential resource that can uplift and empower you.

Moreover, it's important to reciprocate support within your network. Be willing to help others in their endeavors, whether by sharing knowledge, providing introductions, or simply offering encouragement. When you invest in others, you create a cycle of support that can come back to you manifold. Just as the story of John illustrates, where he helped a fellow entrepreneur launch a product, only to later receive invaluable advice that saved his own business, the benefits of building a supportive community are reciprocal.

Finally, leverage technology to expand your network beyond geographical barriers. Online platforms like LinkedIn, community forums, and social media groups can connect you with individuals across the globe. As you build your network, remember to nurture these relationships consistently. Schedule catch-ups, share insights, and celebrate each other's successes. By doing this, you not only strengthen your support system but also lay the groundwork for long-term financial peace and emotional security in your life.

Learning from Others' Financial Journeys

Learning from others' financial journeys offers invaluable insights that can propel us towards our own financial peace.

Each story reveals unique struggles and triumphs, often shedding light on common mistakes that can be avoided. For instance, consider the story of Maria, who, after years of impulsive spending, found herself deep in debt. Through her journey of learning from financial podcasts and connecting with mentors, she not only paid off her debts but also built a substantial savings plan that now supports her dreams.

Understanding the science behind financial behavior can further enhance our learning. Research has shown that individuals who share their financial experiences often foster a community of support that encourages better decision-making. The concept of social learning theory suggests that we learn best when we observe and engage with others. By reflecting on the financial journeys of people around us, we can identify strategies that resonate with our own values and goals.

One of the critical steps in learning from others is actively seeking out stories that align with our aspirations. This could mean reading autobiographies of successful entrepreneurs or joining local financial literacy groups where experiences are shared openly. Take the example of David, who learned the value of budgeting from a friend who meticulously tracked every penny. Inspired by this practice, David adopted a similar method, which ultimately led him to save for his first home much sooner than he expected.

Moreover, it's essential to approach these stories with an open mind. Not every financial journey will mirror our own, and that's a valuable lesson in itself. We can take inspiration from both successes and failures. For example, Jane's experience with stock investments taught her the importance of research and patience. By learning from her mistakes, she became more informed and cautious, eventually leading to her financial independence.

In conclusion, the path to lasting wealth and emotional security is often illuminated by the experiences of others. Embracing stories of financial journeys allows us to reflect on our decisions, adapt strategies, and cultivate a mindset geared towards growth. By integrating these lessons into our lives, we can navigate our financial paths with greater confidence and clarity, ultimately unlocking the peace we seek.

Chapter 9: Taking Action and Staying Committed

Setting Realistic Financial Goals

Setting realistic financial goals is essential for achieving lasting wealth and emotional security. Many people dream of financial independence but often set their sights too high or too low. The journey begins with understanding your current financial situation. This involves assessing your income, expenses, debts, and savings, which can paint a clearer picture of where you stand and where you want to go.

Consider the story of Maria, a single mother who worked multiple jobs to support her family. Initially, she thought she needed to save $50,000 within a year to feel secure. However, after analyzing her finances, she realized that saving $5,000 over five years was more achievable and would still allow her to build a safety net. This shift in perspective not only made her goals more attainable but also reduced her stress, allowing her to focus on her family's well-being.

Research shows that setting specific, measurable, attainable, relevant, and time-bound (SMART) goals significantly increases the likelihood of success. By defining what you want to achieve and breaking it down into smaller, manageable steps, you can create a clear roadmap. For instance, instead of saying, "I want to save money," specify, "I will save $200 each month for the next year to build an emergency fund." This clarity transforms vague aspirations into actionable plans.

Emotional security often stems from having a sense of control over your finances. When setting financial goals, it's crucial to align them with your values and priorities. If travel is important to you, consider saving for a trip instead of pushing it aside for larger, less meaningful goals. This alignment not only keeps you motivated but also enriches your life experiences, making the journey toward financial peace more fulfilling.

Finally, remember that flexibility is key. Life is unpredictable, and your financial goals may need adjustments along the way. Celebrate small victories and don't be discouraged by setbacks. Regularly revisiting and refining your goals ensures that they remain relevant to your life circumstances, helping you to maintain financial peace and emotional security in the long run.

Creating a Long-Term Financial Plan

Creating a long-term financial plan is essential for achieving lasting wealth and emotional security. It begins with understanding your current financial position, including assets, liabilities, income, and expenses. Picture Sarah, a single mother who struggled to manage her finances. By assessing her situation, she realized where her money was going and identified unnecessary expenses that could be cut. This initial step laid the groundwork for her financial transformation.

Next, setting clear financial goals is crucial. These goals should be specific, measurable, attainable, relevant, and time-bound (SMART). For instance, John, a recent college graduate, wanted to save for a home. By defining his goal, he could create a savings plan that was both realistic and motivating. Having a target to work towards gave him the drive to make necessary sacrifices in his spending habits, illustrating the power of goal-setting in financial planning.

A key element in a long-term financial plan is investing wisely. Diversification is a strategy that helps mitigate risks while maximizing returns. Maria, a retiree, learned this lesson after experiencing a market downturn. By spreading her investments across different asset classes, she was able to recover and even grow her wealth over time. Science supports this approach, as studies show that diversified portfolios tend to perform better in the long run, reinforcing the importance of informed investment decisions.

Moreover, regular reviews of your financial plan are necessary to adapt to changing circumstances. Life events such as marriage, having children, or job changes can significantly impact your financial landscape. Consider Tom, who unexpectedly lost his job during a recession. By regularly reviewing his financial plan, he was able to adjust his budget and find alternative income sources, demonstrating resilience and adaptability in the face of challenges.

Lastly, seeking professional advice can provide invaluable insights and guidance. Financial advisors can offer personalized strategies that align with your unique situation and goals. Emily, who felt overwhelmed by her financial choices, sought help from a financial planner. With expert support, she was able to create a solid long-term financial plan that not only secured her future but also brought her peace of mind. This highlights the importance of collaboration in achieving lasting wealth and emotional security.

Staying Motivated Through Challenges

Life frequently presents us with challenges that can test our resolve and motivation. During these times, it is crucial to remember that motivation is not a constant state; it fluctuates based on our circumstances and mindset. A compelling story is that of Thomas Edison, who faced numerous failures before successfully inventing the light bulb. Each setback only fueled his determination, reminding us that persistence is key in overcoming obstacles and achieving our goals.

Scientific research supports the idea that resilience plays a significant role in motivation. Studies show that individuals who maintain a growth mindset are more likely to view challenges as opportunities for development rather than insurmountable barriers. This perspective can transform our approach to difficulties, allowing us to stay focused and motivated even when the odds seem against us. The psychological principle of grit, defined by Angela

Duckworth, emphasizes perseverance and passion for long-term goals, reinforcing the importance of staying the course.

To maintain motivation through challenges, it is essential to set realistic and achievable goals. Breaking down larger objectives into smaller, manageable tasks can create a sense of accomplishment as we progress. This method not only keeps us motivated but also builds momentum. For example, if financial stability is the goal, start by creating a budget or saving a small amount each month. Each step taken is a victory that propels us forward.

Another effective strategy is to cultivate a supportive environment. Surrounding ourselves with positive influences, such as friends, family, or mentors, can provide encouragement during difficult times. Sharing our struggles and successes with others can foster a sense of community and accountability, reminding us that we are not alone in our journey. A powerful anecdote is that of a woman who started a support group for individuals facing financial difficulties, demonstrating how collaboration can help maintain motivation and drive progress.

Lastly, it is important to celebrate small victories along the way. Acknowledging our achievements, no matter how minor, can boost our motivation and reinforce our commitment to our goals. Whether it's treating ourselves to something special or simply taking a moment to reflect on our progress, recognizing our hard work is essential. Remember, staying motivated through challenges is not just about the destination; it is also about appreciating the journey and all the growth that comes with it.

Chapter 10: Celebrating Success and Growth

Recognizing Milestones on the Wealth Journey

Recognizing milestones on your wealth journey is crucial to maintaining motivation and direction. Each milestone acts as a marker of progress, reminding us of how far we have come and the effort we have invested. For instance, consider the story of Sarah, who began her financial journey with overwhelming debt. Over time, she celebrated small victories, such as paying off her first credit card, which ignited her passion for saving and investing. These milestones weren't just numbers; they were symbols of her commitment to changing her financial future.

Science supports the idea that acknowledging milestones enhances our motivation. Research in psychology suggests that setting and recognizing specific goals leads to improved performance and satisfaction. When we celebrate achievements, no matter how small, we release dopamine in our brains, creating a sense of reward and encouraging us to strive for the next goal. This process can be seen in the wealth journey as individuals move from saving small amounts to making significant investments, reinforcing their financial identity and confidence.

To effectively recognize your milestones, consider utilizing a visual tracker, similar to a progress chart used in education. This method allows you to see your advances clearly, whether it's reaching a savings target or successfully budgeting for a vacation. By visually representing your milestones, you create a tangible reminder of your journey, making it easier to stay focused and inspired. For example, John used a simple jar system for his savings, where each filled jar represented a financial goal achieved, creating both visibility and motivation.

Additionally, sharing these milestones with a supportive community can amplify their significance. Engaging with others who are on a similar journey fosters a sense of belonging and accountability. Take the case of a local investment group that meets monthly to share their financial successes. Members celebrate each other's achievements, creating an environment where everyone feels encouraged to strive for their own milestones. This communal recognition not only boosts individual morale but also strengthens the collective commitment to wealth-building.

Lastly, remember that milestones should align with your personal values and long-term vision. Reflect on what wealth means to you beyond financial metrics. Is it about achieving freedom, security, or perhaps the ability to help others? By grounding your milestones in your core values, you ensure that each step taken is meaningful and fulfilling. Celebrate these moments, big or small, as they are all part of your unique wealth journey towards emotional security and lasting peace.

Sharing Your Knowledge and Experiences

Sharing your knowledge and experiences is not only a gift to others but also a pathway to personal growth and financial peace. When we open up about our journeys, we create connections that resonate deeply with those around us. For instance, consider the story of a retired teacher who, after years of financial struggle, decided to share her expertise in budgeting with her community. Her workshops not only transformed her own financial outlook but also empowered countless individuals to take control of their finances.

Research supports the idea that sharing knowledge leads to a deeper understanding of the subject matter. When we teach others, we reinforce our own understanding and often discover new insights in the process. A study published in the Journal of Financial Planning found that individuals who mentor others about financial literacy experience a greater sense of financial confidence themselves. This reciprocal relationship highlights the importance of community in achieving lasting wealth.

One effective step in sharing your knowledge is to start small. Host a casual gathering with friends or family where you can discuss financial strategies that worked for you. Share your successes and failures, and encourage open dialogue. By creating a safe space for discussion, you not only contribute to the collective knowledge but also foster an environment where everyone feels comfortable learning and growing together.

As you become more comfortable sharing, consider expanding your reach. Utilize social media platforms or community forums to share your experiences and lessons learned. You might write a blog post detailing your journey through financial decisions or create informative videos on budgeting techniques. The more you share, the more you inspire others to embark on their own journeys toward financial peace.

Finally, remember that sharing is not just about imparting wisdom; it's also about listening. Engage with those who seek your guidance and encourage them to share their stories as well. This exchange of experiences not only enriches your perspective but also builds a supportive network. Together, through shared knowledge and experiences, we can unlock the doors to lasting wealth and emotional security for ourselves and others.

Continuing the Cycle of Wealth and Emotional Security

In the journey towards lasting wealth and emotional security, understanding the cycle of wealth is pivotal. This cycle begins with the decisions we make about our finances, influenced by our values and beliefs. For instance, consider the story of a young couple who, after years of spending impulsively, decided to adopt a budgeting plan. Over time, their diligent efforts not only improved their financial situation but also fostered a deeper emotional connection, proving that financial decisions are deeply intertwined with emotional well-being.

Science supports the idea that financial stability contributes significantly to emotional security. Research indicates that individuals with a solid financial foundation report higher levels of happiness and lower levels of stress. This connection is evident in stories of families who, after establishing a savings plan, felt a newfound sense of security. They could face unexpected challenges—like medical emergencies or job losses—without the paralyzing fear that often accompanies financial instability.

Continuing the cycle of wealth also involves teaching the next generation about financial literacy. When parents share their financial journeys, including successes and failures, they empower their children to make informed decisions. For example, a father who shares his experience of overcoming debt teaches his child the importance of budgeting and saving. This knowledge not only helps the child secure their future but also reinforces the family's emotional bonds, as they navigate financial challenges together.

Moreover, it is essential to recognize that wealth is not solely about money but encompasses emotional richness as well. Engaging in community service or supporting local businesses can create a ripple effect that enhances both personal and communal wealth. Stories abound of individuals who found joy and fulfillment in giving back, thereby enriching their own lives while contributing to the welfare of others. This interconnectedness is a testament to the cycle of wealth that thrives on generosity and shared prosperity.

To sustain this cycle, individuals must regularly reassess their financial goals and emotional needs. Setting aside time for reflection allows one to align their wealth decisions with their core values. A woman who reevaluates her spending habits to prioritize experiences over material possessions often finds greater joy and satisfaction. As we continue this cycle, we not only build our own financial peace but also create a legacy of emotional security for those who come after us. Its a beaufiful day

www.ingramcontent.com/pod-product-compliance
Lightning Source LLC
LaVergne TN
LVHW022321200926
848481LV00004B/1382